Catching Randy the Rainbow Trout

Written by John Jensen
Illustrated by Randy Gates

Copyright © 2013 B.F.S, Inc.
All rights reserved.

ISBN: 0615793096
ISBN 13: 9780615793092

Printed and bound in the United States of America

First printing 2013

All rights reserved. No part of this book may be reproduced or transmitted in any form or by any means, electronic or mechanical, including photocopying, recording or by an information storage and retrieval system- except by a reviewer who may quote brief passages in a review to be printed in a magazine, newspaper or on the Web- without permission in writing from the publisher.

DEDICATION

My thanks to God for inspiring my twin passions
of Bible Study and fly fishing.
I dedicate this book to my wife and favorite fishing partner
Anna Dee,
our beautiful and talented daughter and son Sara and Bob,
their rascally sons Will and Wyatt,
the Backseat Coyote Club,
the PCBW Fishing Posse,
and to Papa Don Jensen who started me fly fishing.

"Catching Randy the Rainbow Trout"
A Will and Wyatt Adventure
Text by John Jensen. Illustrations by Randall Gates.
Edited by Sara Howard, Computer consulting by Michael Brady
For information contact:
John Jensen (jensenjohn64@gmail.com)
P.O. Box 4050, Hailey, Idaho 83333

It was a blue bird morning when Will and Wyatt found their grandpa reading his Bible. "Papa," they said, "will you take us fishing?"

"What a great idea!" said Papa. "I'll introduce you to Randy the Rainbow Trout and his trout friends. Randy is the biggest trout in the Big Wood River, and I have a special fly we can use to catch him."

The boys' eyes opened wide, excited for their adventure to begin! Papa told the boys to get on their fishing clothes, and then went to the garage to get their fishing gear ready. He was excited for the boys to catch fish, and be with them out in God's playground!

While working in her kitchen, Grandma Nana overheard the conversation about the fishermen's plan. She prepared them a delicious snack and put it in a backpack. As Nana gave Papa the pack she said, "Be careful walking down the trail to the river. Will, you watch Wyatt closely; he's younger than you and may need some help. When you come home, I want to hear all about the special day you three have!"

Papa, Will and Wyatt each kissed Nana on the cheek as a thank you for being so nice, then off they went to the river.

The trail to the river was through a grove of cottonwood and aspen trees, with meadow grasses and special summer flowers. As they walked, they talked about which of the flowers was most beautiful. They decided wild daisies were the best because they looked the happiest!

Will helped his brother Wyatt on the trail, holding his hand and leading him along. Loving brothers watching out for each other! Sunlight through the tall trees warmed their backs and made them thirsty. "Papa, can I please have a drink of water?" asked Wyatt.

"Of course you can," said Papa. "We're almost at the river. I'll dig the canteen of water out of our pack when we get there."

At the river, Papa told Will and Wyatt the story of Randy the Rainbow Trout as they all had a drink of water. "Do you see that big log on the far side of the river, and the deep pool beside it? That is where Randy the Rainbow Trout lives. He is the biggest and smartest rainbow trout around."

"When God made Randy, he made his rainbow with bright red and pink colors. His back is bluish green and speckled with little black dots. The tips of his fins are pearly white. All in all, the best looking fish in the river, and the heaviest. He's a whopper! If one of you boys hooks him while fishing, you're in for quite a battle. I've only caught Randy once this year. It was such a battle that my arm was sore for two whole days from the fight!"

Will said to Papa, "You told us about a special fly we could fish with today. Do you have more than one so we can all fish at once?"

Papa laughed, "Oh Will, you know I have a big box full of flies! I have plenty for everyone. I'm the fishing guide today, and I'll teach you two boys a secret trick to use in catching big rainbow trout."

Papa put the fishing rods together, strung the lines on the rods, and then tied on each his special Green Drake fly. He crimped the barbs on the hooks, so they wouldn't hurt the fish they were sure to catch.

Will and Wyatt were so excited thinking about battling whopper rainbow trout!

Papa gave them their rods and said, "Last night and early this morning all the rainbow trout have been sleeping on the bottom of the river. Now that the sun is up, the trout have decided they're hungry.   If we show them a big fly, they will gobble it for breakfast. Let's walk in the water a little way. It is cold and will feel good."

Will and Wyatt took their fishing rods, but didn't know where to start fishing. Papa saw that Wyatt was slipping on the round, mossy rocks so he took Wyatt by the hand to help him wade in the water.

"Will," Papa said, "you walk up the stream to where the water gathers in front of that big log where Randy the Rainbow Trout lives.   Cast your fly up stream and let it float a long way on the water before it gets by the big log!"

"Float the fly next to the log, making it look like it wants to climb out of the water on to the log. That might make Randy think his breakfast is getting away, and he'll strike your fly. That's my secret trick! I'll help your brother fish at the bottom of the deep pool where the smaller fish live."

Papa and Wyatt held hands wading in the water. As soon as Wyatt cast his fly on the water, a hungry rainbow trout jumped out of the water to eat the fly. He caught the fly in his mouth!

"Pull back and set the hook Wyatt," Papa said loudly. Wyatt pulled back, and hooked the rainbow trout just like Papa said to do.   Oh what fun Wyatt had, as the rainbow trout jumped and swam around in the river!

"Hold the tip of your rod up high Wyatt," said Papa as the rainbow trout fought harder and harder. Wyatt was very brave and strong. Soon the rainbow trout tired of the fight and swam over near Wyatt and Papa.

Papa reached down and held the beautiful rainbow trout in his hand. "Look closely at this rainbow trout, Wyatt, and appreciate what a great gift he is to us from God! Isn't he beautiful?"

"Beautiful like rainbows after a rainstorm, only we don't have to get wet to enjoy him!" said Wyatt. "I feel like Noah in the flood story you told us, grateful for my own special rainbow."

Papa took the fly out of the rainbow trout's mouth and let him swim away, back to the bottom of the pool in the river. Wyatt smiled and said, "Yahoo!" He was a very happy little boy!

While Wyatt was catching his rainbow trout, Will was casting his fly on the water, at the place where the water gathered in front of the big log and deep pool, where Randy the Rainbow Trout lives. Several times his fly floated towards the log, only to sink under the water.

Will heard Papa yell, "Will, try casting a little farther up stream and further out." Will expertly cast the fly just like Papa told him. As the fly danced on the water towards the log, Will was sure it would go under the water, but it did not. Will was very excited as he saw the fly floating next to the big log, which was Papa's secret trick! Will couldn't believe his eyes, as he saw a huge dark fish swimming up from the bottom of the deep pool towards his fly!

Suddenly, the Green Drake fly disappeared into the mouth of the biggest rainbow trout Will had ever seen. It was Randy the Rainbow Trout for sure, and he was eating Will's fly! Will pulled back on his fly rod, setting the hook into Randy's mouth.

Will knew that Randy would try to break his line on the branches, so with all his strength he pulled the fishing rod to the right to force Randy away from the branches. Will started to slip on the mossy rocks, but regained his balance. What a tremendous battle between Will and Randy!

Papa and Wyatt ran up the river to watch Will land his great fish! Wyatt was so proud of his strong older brother. Will fought the huge fish for a long time. Finally, Randy swam over to Will's feet. Papa put his hand under the large fish and released it from the hook!

"Have you boys ever seen such a beautiful fish?" asked Papa as he held Randy out of the water. "Never!" said the boys in unison. "God has given us a special memory today," said Papa as he released Randy the Rainbow Trout back into the Big Wood River.

Papa, Will and Wyatt smiled at each other. "Let's eat the snack that Nana made for us," said Will. "I'm hungry." "Me too," said Wyatt. Papa took Wyatt's hand and helped him out of the water and on to the bank of the river.

As they ate and laughed and talked about the adventure stories they would tell Nana, Papa said, "We certainly shared a lot of love today, from Nana taking care of us to you brothers watching out for each other, to even God loving us in giving us rainbow trout to catch!" Will replied, "Papa, don't forget about you sharing your love of fly fishing with us!"

Be Intentional…….

To fly fish is to be intentional about Joy. You must also be intentional in sharing what is most meaningful in your life, with those who mean the most to you. If the life lessons found in the Bible are valuable to you, then be intentional in both sharing them with family and making them relevant in their lives. For example, you can share Noah's story from Genesis 6 - 8 and why it is important from Hebrews 11. And you can share the wisdom of the Ten Commandments as found in Exodus 20, and that is good. You should also apply this same wisdom in teaching the rules of fishing:

- Frequently look up from the water to appreciate the beauty of your surroundings. God made these special places for you to visit.

- Fly fishing is great fun, however it is only one blessed gift in this life. Never let fishing totally consume you.

- At times fish are hard to catch. And sometimes they get away before you can land them. That's fishing! Don't be upset and say bad words.

- You will feel God's presence while fishing. To really talk to God on the stream, you must put down your rod, be still, then listen to Him.

🐟 Appreciate with love those who share their fly fishing skills with you. Respect them by freely sharing those same skills with others.

🐟 De-barb your hooks. Only keep the fish you intend to eat; catch and release the rest.

🐟 If your fishing companion is catching more fish than you, be happy for them and not grumpy.

🐟 Respect all fishing laws and regulations about licensing, seasons and limits.   Stay out of private water unless you have permission to be there.

🐟 As much as possible, be truthful about size and number of fish caught.

🐟 There is always lots of water to fish.   Never be upset if someone is in your favorite run.

And if you believe in Jesus Christ, share your faith and so become a fisher of men!

www.ingramcontent.com/pod-product-compliance
Lightning Source LLC
Chambersburg PA
CBHW041537040426
42446CB00002B/124